Fabulous Animal Facts

That Hardly Anyone Knows

by Rita Golden Gelman

Illustrated by Margaret A. Hartelius

SCHOLASTIC INC.

New York Toronto London Auckland Sydney

For Danielle

ISBN 0-590-30561-1

Copyright © 1981 by S & R Gelman Associates, Inc. All rights reserved. Published by Scholastic Inc.

12 11 10 9 8 7 6 5 4 3 2   7 8 9/8 0 1/9

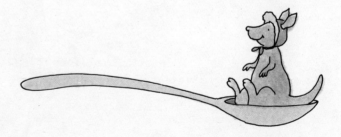

A newborn baby kangaroo can fit in a teaspoon.
It is less than one inch long.

A newborn baby blue whale is 25 feet long.
It would just about fit in a bus.

When a snake or lizard or bird is inside its egg,

it grows an egg tooth.

When the baby is ready to come out,

it uses its egg tooth to crack the shell.

For the tooth fairy!

Once the baby is out, it doesn't need

its egg tooth anymore.

The tooth falls off.

Two days before a baby chick hatches,
you can sometimes hear it peep
right through the shell.

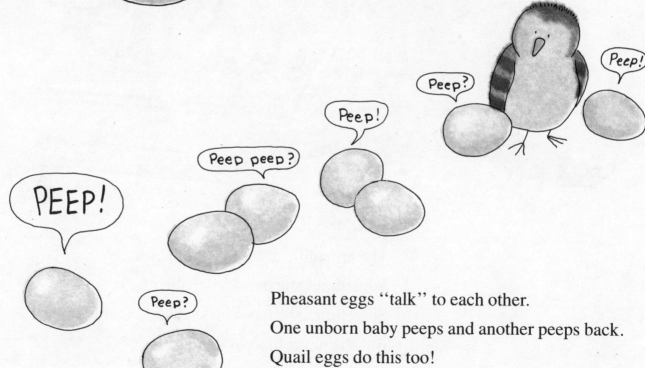

Pheasant eggs "talk" to each other.
One unborn baby peeps and another peeps back.
Quail eggs do this too!

The armadillo always has 4 babies.

Sometimes she has 4 boy babies.

Sometimes she has 4 girl babies.

But she never has boys and girls

at the same time.

Every spring the female codfish lays
about 5 million eggs.

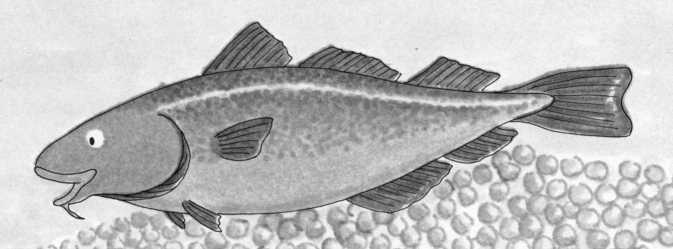

One female housefly lays more than
100 eggs at a time.
The eggs hatch in less than two days.
The babies grow quickly.
In only two weeks, the 50 or more female
babies can lay their own eggs.

I started the
whole thing!

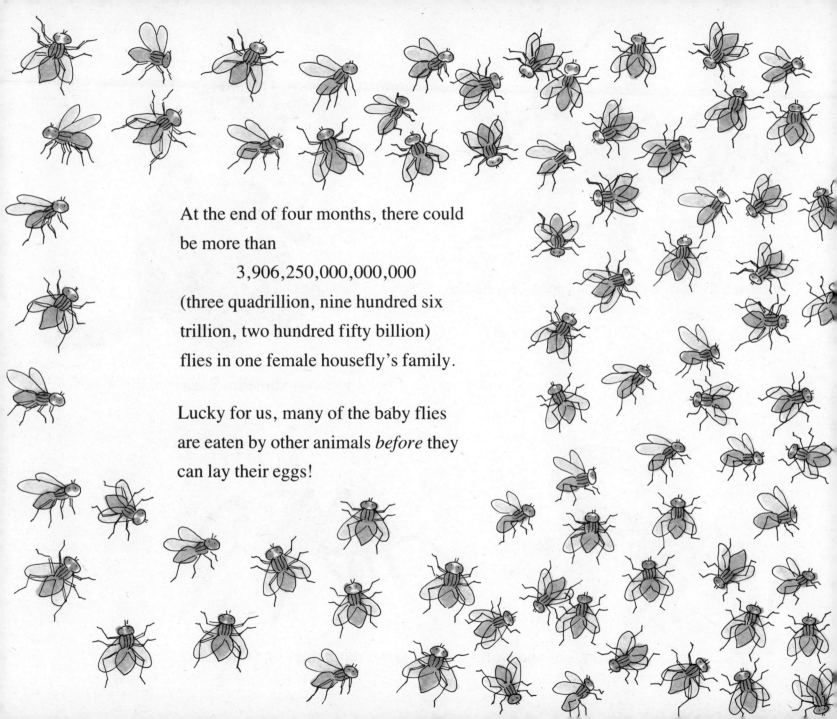

At the end of four months, there could
be more than
     3,906,250,000,000,000
(three quadrillion, nine hundred six
trillion, two hundred fifty billion)
flies in one female housefly's family.

Lucky for us, many of the baby flies
are eaten by other animals *before* they
can lay their eggs!

Crayfish babies ride on their mothers' stomachs.

Beavers sometimes carry their babies in their arms.

Scorpions and wolf spiders carry their babies on their backs.

A polar bear mother takes her baby
for swimming rides.

Baby bats go for flying rides.

A hummingbird can flap its wings 80 times
in one second.

The hummingbird is like a helicopter.
It can fly up.
It can fly down.
It can fly forward and backward.
It can even stay in one place.

The hummingbird is lucky it can do
all those things in the air.
It can barely walk.

The albatross is like a kite.
It can ride the sea winds all day
without flapping its wings.

Monkeys hang by their tails.

Sloths walk upside down.
They even eat upside down.

One kind of skunk stands on its hands
when it is afraid.
It can stay up for more than 6 seconds.

A sea otter swims on its back.

Sometimes it balances a rock on its stomach.

If it feels like having a snack,

it bangs a shellfish on the rock

until the shellfish breaks open.

Then the otter can eat while it floats.

Sometimes the sea otter wants to rest on its back.

But it doesn't want to float away.

It makes an anchor.

It wraps itself up in seaweed

that is attached to the bottom.

Then the otter can rest

and stay in the same place.

Bee babies eat 23 meals a day.

Hummingbirds eat more than 60 meals a day.

An elephant eats more in one week than many
people eat in a year.

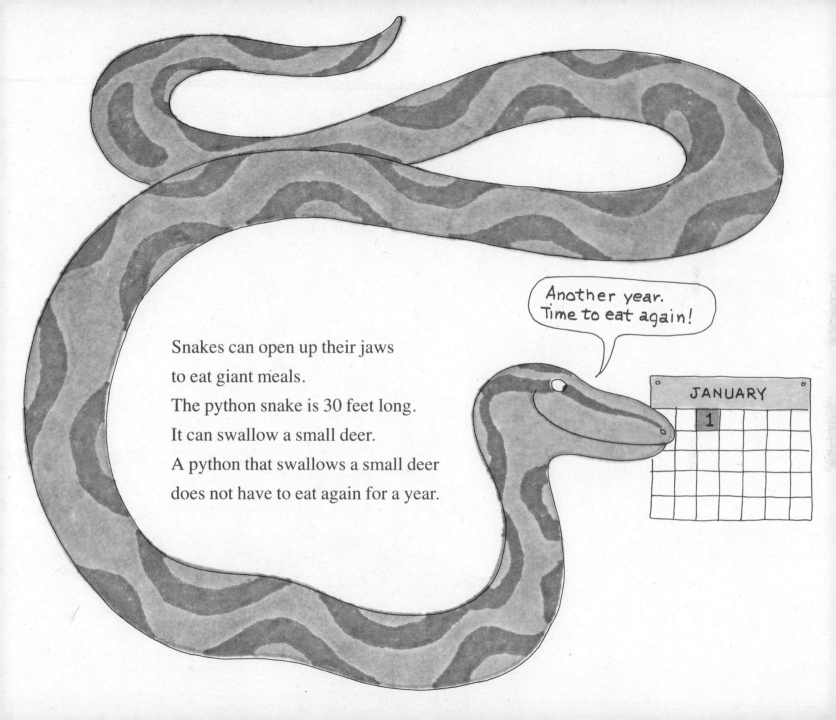

Snakes can open up their jaws
to eat giant meals.
The python snake is 30 feet long.
It can swallow a small deer.
A python that swallows a small deer
does not have to eat again for a year.

The gray whale has brush-like strainers
instead of teeth.
It opens its mouth and gulps a lot of water.
Then it closes its mouth and squirts the
water through the strainers.
When the water is gone,
the whale has a mouthful of dinner.

Flamingoes have strainers too.
They gulp a mouthful of muddy water
and squirt it through the strainers.
Tiny plants and animals get caught
in the strainers.
Then the flamingo eats its dinner.

Flamingoes eat a lot of brine shrimp.
The shrimp have pink coloring in them.
The more shrimp a flamingo eats,
the pinker it gets.

One kind of finch eats with a toothpick.

Its favorite food lives in holes in a tree.

But its beak isn't long enough

to get into the hole.

So the finch picks a cactus needle 2 inches long.

It sticks the needle into the hole.

It spears the food and pulls out dinner.

Some vultures eat ostrich eggs.

But ostrich eggs have very hard shells.

The vultures cannot break the shells with their beaks.

The vultures throw stones at the eggs.

They miss about half the time.

But they keep trying until the eggs crack.

Honey ants eat a sweet liquid
called honey dew.
They take it home and feed it
to special ants in the nest.
The special ants are living storage tanks.
They store up so much honey dew
that they can hardly move.
They just hang from the ceiling by tiny claws.

A hungry ant can put its mouth
next to the mouth of a storage ant
and collect a drop of honey dew
for dinner.

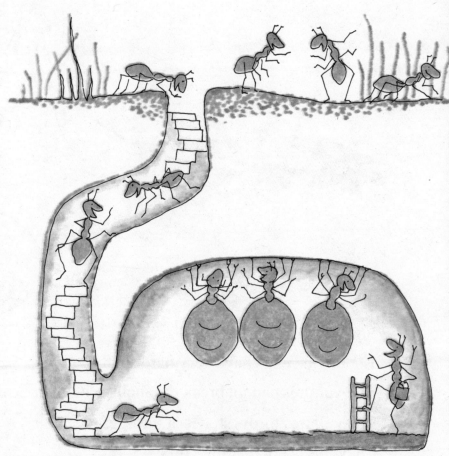

A camel is also a living storage tank.

Its hump is a big lump of fat.

If the camel has no food, it uses the fat
in its hump for energy.

Sometimes the camel uses so much fat
that the hump slips off its back onto its side.

When the camel eats again,
the hump returns.

Lantern fish live near the bottom of the ocean.

It is very dark down there.

Lantern fish carry their own lights.

The lights look like tiny pearls.

They are called photophores.

A lantern fish can flash its photophores on and off.

A lantern fish gives off enough light

to light up a dark room.

The angler fish fishes for its dinner.

It has a rod, a line, a float, and lighted bait.

The bait can flash yellow, green, and orange.

The "lights" are really tiny bacteria
that are inside the fish.

The lighted bait attracts curious fish
who soon become dinner for the angler.

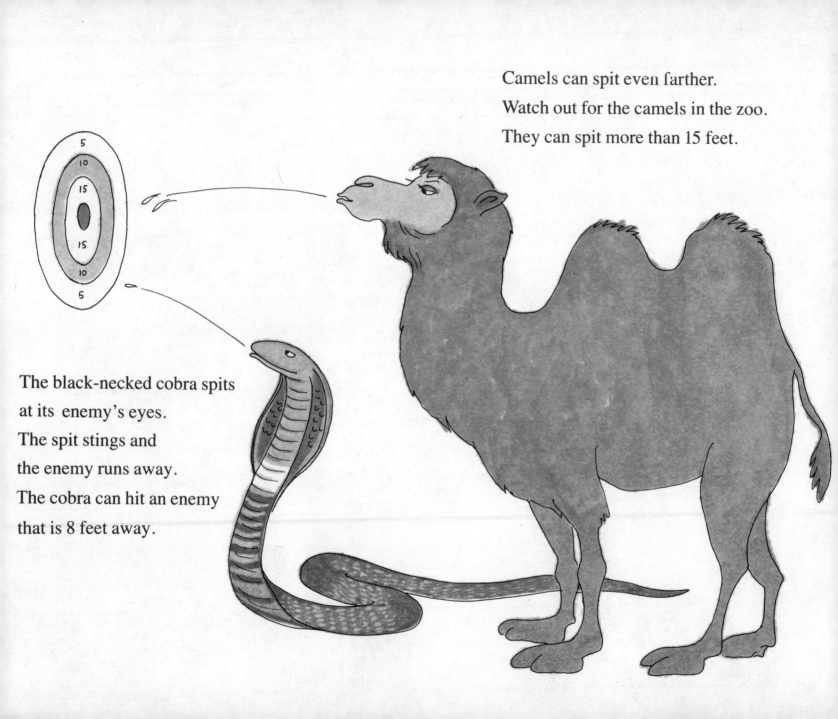

Camels can spit even farther.
Watch out for the camels in the zoo.
They can spit more than 15 feet.

The black-necked cobra spits
at its enemy's eyes.
The spit stings and
the enemy runs away.
The cobra can hit an enemy
that is 8 feet away.

The bombing beetle has a special
opening in its body that can shoot liquid.
The beetle can squirt 29 times in
just 4 minutes.

The archer fish can spit at an insect
that is 3 feet away.
When the insect is hit, it falls into
the water and becomes dinner for the fish.

A weasel is brown in the summer
So is the Arctic fox.

In winter they both grow new white
coats to match the season.

An octopus can change its color
in less than a second.
As it walks along the bottom,
it can turn from white to yellow
to red to brown.
It can even make stripes and polka dots.

If a lizard is caught by the tail,
the tail may snap off.
The broken-off tail wiggles and
squiggles while the lizard escapes.

When a lizard loses its tail,
it grows a new one.

The tail of a field mouse
sometimes gets broken off too.
But it won't grow back.

Every year in December or January,
a deer's antlers fall off.
A few months later, new antlers grow.
The new antlers are always bigger than
the old ones.

Antelopes, sheep and rhinoceroses
don't have antlers.
They have horns.
If a horn breaks off, it doesn't grow back.

Elephant tusks are not antlers or horns.

They are teeth.

Some elephant tusks are 8 feet long.

Many elephants have a favorite tusk.

They are right-tusked or left-tusked,

just as people are right-handed or

left-handed.

Full grown birds change
all their feathers every year.
Most do it gradually,
a few feathers at a time.

Ducks, geese and swans
shed their *flight* feathers all at once.
When their *flight* feathers are off
these birds can't fly.
They have to hide from their enemies.

Every 6 months, a snake crawls out of its skin.

The snake crawls over rocks and bushes and grass
until the loose skin peels off.

The skin comes off inside out and in one piece.

Then the snake crawls away in its new skin.

Some lizards change their skins once a month.

Horses and giraffes sleep standing up.

Bats sleep upside down.

Fish sleep with their eyes open.
So do snakes.

Birds have special muscles
that lock their claws to branches.
That way they can sleep all night
without ever falling off.

Hippos sleep in a big heap.
They use each other as pillows.

That's all for now. Good-night!